9+ CONQUER Comprehension

BOOK 1

Building confidence for budding learners

Published by SVR Education Ltd

First published in 2018

ISBN. 9781999899196

Author Sheila Robinson
Design Phil Tristram
Editor Tom Stevens
Contributors Annie Leslie, Fiona Swann
Cover illustration Stuart Lynch
Printed by Tadberry Evedale

1

The Iron Man

BY TED HUGHES

The Iron Man came to the top of the cliff.

How far had he walked? Nobody knows. Where had he come from? Nobody knows. How was he made? Nobody knows.

Taller than a house, the Iron Man stood at the top of the cliff, on the very brink, in the darkness.

The wind sang through his iron fingers. His great iron head, shaped like a dustbin but as big as a bedroom, slowly turned to the right, slowly turned to the left. His iron ears turned, this way, that way. He was hearing the sea. His eyes, like headlamps, glowed white, then red, then infra-red, searching the sea. Never before had the Iron Man seen the sea.

He swayed in the strong wind that pressed against his back. He swayed forward, on the brink of the high cliff.

And his right foot, his enormous iron right foot, lifted – up, out into space, and the Iron Man stepped forward, off the cliff, into nothingness.

CRRRAAAASSSSSSH!

Down the cliff the Iron Man came toppling, head over heels.

CRASH!

CRASH!

CRASH!

From rock to rock, snag to snag, tumbling slowly. And as he crashed and crashed and crashed his iron legs fell off.

His iron arms broke off, and the hands broke off the arms.

His great iron ears fell off and his eyes fell out.

His great iron head fell off.

All the separate pieces tumbled, scattered, crashing, bumping, clanging, down on to the rocky beach far below.

A few rocks tumbled with him.

Then

Silence.

Only the sound of the sea, chewing away at the edge of the rocky beach, where the bits and pieces of the Iron Man lay scattered far and wide, silent and unmoving.

Only one of the iron hands, lying beside an old sand-logged washed-up seaman's boot, waved its fingers for a minute, like a crab on its back. Then it lay still.

While the stars went on wheeling through the sky and the wind went on tugging at the grass on the cliff-top and the sea went on boiling and booming.

Nobody knew the Iron Man had fallen.

Night passed.

Just before dawn, as the darkness grew blue and the shapes of the rocks separated from each other, two seagulls flew crying over the rocks. They landed on a patch of sand. They had two chicks in a nest on the cliff. Now they were searching for food.

One of the seagulls flew up – Aaaaaark! He had seen something. He glided low over the sharp rocks. He landed and picked something up. Something shiny, round and hard. It was one of the Iron Man's eyes. He brought it back to his mate. They both looked at this strange thing. And the eye looked at them. It rolled from side to side looking first at one gull, then at the other. The gulls, peering at it, thought it was a strange kind of clam, peeping at them from its shell.

Then the other gull flew up, wheeled around and landed and picked something up. Some awkward, heavy thing. The gull flew low and slowly, dragging the heavy thing. Finally, the gull dropped it beside the eye. This new thing had five legs. It moved. The gulls thought it was a strange kind of crab. They thought they had found a strange crab and a strange clam. They did not know they had found the Iron Man's eye and the Iron Man's right hand.

But as soon as the eye and the hand got together the eye looked at the hand. Its light glowed blue. The hand stood up on three fingers and its thumb, and craned its forefinger like a long nose. It felt around. It touched the eye. Gleefully it picked up the eye, and tucked it under its middle finger. The eye peered out, between the forefinger and thumb. Now the hand could see.

It looked around. Then it darted and jabbed one of the gulls with its stiffly held finger, then darted at the other and jabbed him. The two gulls flew up into the wind with a frightened cry.

Extract from *The Iron Man* by Ted Hughes

QUESTIONS (Answer in Full Sentences)

1 How does the author create suspense and mystery in the first few lines?

2 What is compared to the Iron Man's size?

3 Give two examples of similes from the passage.

4 Give three words that describe how the Iron Man might have felt.

5 What sounds could be heard once the Iron Man had fallen?

6 How did the Iron Man's fingers wave?

7 Which phrase in the passage describes the weather?

8 When did the seagulls fly over the rocks?

9 Why were they searching for food?

10 What did the gulls mistake the Iron Man's eye for?

2

Once

BY MORRIS GLEITZMAN

I reach into my shirt and after a struggle because a couple of other people's elbows are in my chest I manage to pull out my notebook and rip out a couple of blank pages.

'Here,' I say to the woman in the corner. 'Use this.'

The other people pass it over to her and when she sees what it is she starts crying.

'It's alright,' I say, 'I haven't written on it.'

Barney squeezes my arm.

'Well done, Felix,' he says.

Lots of other people hold their hands out for toilet paper and I rip pages out for them as well. Now I've only got pages left with stories on them. Stories I wrote about Mum and Dad.

I look over at the people crouching in the corner, at the relief on their faces.

Mum and Dad would understand.

I rip the rest of the pages out of my notebook and wriggle past everyone to the toilet corner. I grab a metal bolt poking out of a plank in the wall. If I push the bolt through the pages, they'll hang there and people can tear off a page or two as they need them.

The bolt comes away in my hands.

The wooden plank is rotten.

I kick at it and part of my foot goes through.

'Barney,' I yell.

People are looking at what I've done. A couple of men pull my foot out of the plank and start kicking at the wood themselves. Their big boots make a much bigger hole.

Barney and the men pull at the side of the hole with their hands and more bolts fly out of the wood and suddenly the whole plank comes away.

I can see green countryside speeding past. One of the men tries to squeeze through.

'Wait,' says Barney. 'We need to make the hole bigger. If you roll out you'll fall on the track. You need to be able to jump clear.'

Everyone squashes back to give Barney and the men more room. Barney jams the plank into the hole and the men push till their faces are bulging.

A second plank splinters and the men kick it out.

They do the same with a third.

'That's enough,' yells one of the men. He takes a couple of steps back and dives out through the hole. The second man follows him.

'Come on,' yells someone else. 'We're free.'

More people fling themselves through the hole.

I grab Barney.

'Won't the Nazis stop the train and catch them?' I say.

Barney shakes his head. 'They won't let anything interfere with their timetable,' he says. 'They don't need to.'

We all freeze, startled, as gunshots echo through the train.

Lots of gunshots.

'They've got machine guns on the roof,' says Barney, hugging the little kids to him. 'Easier for them than stopping the train.'

People are peering out of the hole, trying to see what happened to the ones who jumped.

'Look,' screams a woman. 'Some of them have made it. They're running into the woods. They're free.'

I grab Barney again.

'We've got to risk it,' I say.

I can see Barney doesn't agree. I can see why. Henryk and Janek are in tears. Ruth and Jacob are clinging to each other, terrified. Moshe has stopped chewing his wood.

I crouch down and in as calm a voice as I can, I tell them a story. It's a story about some kids who jump off a train and land in a soft meadow and a farmer comes and takes them home and they live happily on the farm with his family and get very good at growing vegetables and in the year 1972 they invent a carrot that cures all illnesses.

I pull Zelda's carrot out of my pocket to show them it's possible.

But I can see that most of them aren't convinced.

'Felix,' says Barney. 'If you want to risk it, I won't stop you. But I have to stay with the ones who don't want to.'

'No,' I say, pleading. 'We all have to jump.'

Extract from *Once* by Morris Gleitzman

QUESTIONS (Answer in Full Sentences)

1 What does Felix pull from his notebook?

2 Why does Barney squeeze Felix's arm?

3 Why does the bolt come away in Felix's hands?

4 What made the hole bigger?

5 What can Felix see through the hole?

6 Why does the hole need to be bigger?

7 How does Felix try to calm the children?

8 Write a paragraph about the mood of the scene on the train?

9 What did Felix have in his pocket?

10 What was on the roof of the train?

3

The Firework-Maker's Daughter

BY PHILIP PULLMAN

Now the king of that country owned a White Elephant. It was custom that whenever the King wanted to punish one of his courtiers, he would send him the White Elephant as a present, and the expense of looking after the animal would ruin the poor man; because the White Elephant had to sleep between silk sheets (enormous ones), and eat mango-flavoured Turkish Delight (tons of it), and have his tusks covered in gold leaf every morning. When the courtier had no money left at all, the White Elephant would be returned to the King, ready for his next victim.

Wherever the White Elephant went, his personal servant had to go too. The servant's name was Chulak, and he was the same age as Lila. In fact, they were friends.

Every afternoon Chulak would take the White Elephant out for his exercise, because the Elephant would go with no-one else, and there was a reason for this: Chulak was the only person, besides Lila, who knew that the Elephant could talk.

One day Lila went to visit Chulak and the White Elephant. She arrived at the Elephant House in time to hear the Elephant Master losing his temper.

'You horrible little boy!' he roared. 'You've done it again, haven't you?'

'Done what?' said Chulak innocently.

'Look!' said the Elephant Master, pointing with a quivering finger at the White Elephant's snowy flanks.

Written all over his side in charcoal and paint were dozens of slogans:

EAT AT THE GOLDEN LANTERN

BANGKOK WANDERERS FOR THE CUP

STAR OF INDIA TANDOORI HOUSE

And right at the very top of the White Elephant's back in great big letters:

CHANG LOVES LOTUS BLOSSOM TRUE XXX

'Every day this Elephant comes home with graffiti all over him!' shouted the Elephant Master. 'Why don't you stop people doing it?'

'I can't understand how it happens, Master,' said Chulak. 'Mind you, the traffic's awful. I've got to watch those rickshaw-drivers like a hawk. I can't look out for graffiti artists as well – they just slap it up and run.'

'But Chang loves Lotus Blossom True must have taken a good ten minutes on a stepladder!'

'Yes, it's a mystery to me, Master. Shall I clean it off?'

'All of it! There's a job coming up in a day or two, and I want this animal clean.'

And the Elephant Master stormed off, leaving Chulak and Lila with the Elephant.

'Hello, Hamlet,' said Lila.

'Hello, Lila,' said the Elephant. 'Look what this obnoxious brat has reduced me to! A walking billboard!'

'Stop fussing,' said Chulak. 'Look, we've got eighteen rupees already – and ten annas from the Tandoori House – and Chang gave me a whole rupee for letting him write that on the top. We're nearly there, Hamlet!'

'The shame!' said Hamlet, shaking his great head.

'You mean you charge people money to write on him?' said Lila.

'Course!' said Chulak. 'It's dead lucky to write your name on a White Elephant. When we've got enough, we're going to run away. Trouble is, he's in love with a lady elephant at the zoo. You ought to see him blush when we go past – like a ton of strawberry ice cream!'

Extract from *The Firework-Maker's Daughter* by Philip Pullman

QUESTIONS (Answer in Full Sentences)

1 What was the King's custom?

2 Why was the White Elephant a curse on the courtiers?

3 What expensive habits did the White Elephant have? Name three.

4 Who was the White Elephant's servant?

5 Give two examples of graffiti written on the elephant's body.

6 Why did only Chulak and Lila take the White Elephant for a walk?

7 Which word in the passage means shaking?

8 How was the graffiti applied to the White Elephant?

9 What were Chulak's motives for the graffiti?

10 Find an example of a simile in the passage.

4

Tom's Midnight Garden

BY PHILIPPA PEARCE

This was a real expedition. Tom put on his bedroom slippers, but decided against his dressing-gown: after all, it was summer. He closed his bedroom door carefully behind him, so that it should not bang in his absence. Outside the front door of the flat he took off one of his slippers; he laid it on the floor against the door jamb and then closed the door on to it, as on to a wedge. That would keep the door open for his return.

The lights on the first-floor landing and in the hall were turned out, for the tenants were all in bed and asleep, and Mrs Bartholomew was asleep and dreaming. The only illumination was a sideways shaft of moonlight through the long window part way up the stairs. Tom felt his way downstairs and into the hall.

Here he was checked. He could find the grandfather clock – a tall and ancient figure of black in the lesser blackness – but he was unable to read its face. If he opened its dial-door and felt until he found the position of the clock-hands, then his sense of touch would tell him the time. He fumbled first at one side of the door, then at the other; but there seemed no catch – no way in. He remembered how the pendulum-case door had not yielded to him either, on that first day. Both must be kept locked.

Hurry! hurry! The house seemed to whisper round him. The hour is passing... passing...

Tom turned from the clock to feel for the electric-light switch. Where had it been? His fingers swept the walls in vain: nowhere.

Light – light: that was what he needed! And the only light was the moonbeam that glanced sideways through the stairway window and spent itself at once and uselessly on the wall by the window-sill.

Tom studied the moonbeam, with an idea growing in his mind. From the direction in which the beam came, he saw that the moon must be shining at the back of the house. Very well then, if he opened the door at the far end of the hall – at the back of the house, that is – he would let that moonlight in. With luck there might be enough light for him to read the clock-face.

He moved down the hall to the door at its far end. It was a door he had never seen opened – the Kitsons used the door at the front. They said that the door at the back was only a less convenient way to the street, through a back-yard – a strip of paving where dustbins were kept and where the tenants of the ground-floor back flat garaged their car under tarpaulin.

Never having had occasion to use the door, Tom had no idea how it might be secured at night. If it were locked, and the key kept elsewhere... But it was not locked, he found; only bolted. He drew the bolt and, very slowly, to make no sound, turned the door-knob.

Hurry! whispered the house; and the grandfather clock at the heart of it beat an anxious tick, tick.

Tom opened the door wide and let in the moonlight. It flooded in, as bright as daylight – the white daylight that comes before the full rising of the sun. The illumination was perfect, but Tom did not at once turn to see what it showed him of the clock-face. Instead he took a step forward on to the doorstep. He was staring, at first in surprise, then with indignation, at what he saw outside. That they should have deceived him – lied to him – like this! They had said, 'It's not worth your while going out at the back, Tom.' So carelessly they had described it: 'A sort of back-yard, very poky, with rubbish bins. Really, there's nothing to see.'

Nothing... Only this: a great lawn where flower-beds bloomed; a towering fir-tree, and thick, beetle-browed yews that humped their shapes down two sides of the lawn; on the third side, to the right, a greenhouse almost the size of a real house; from each corner of the lawn, a path that twisted away to some other depths of garden, with other trees.

Extract from *Tom's Midnight Garden* by Philippa Pearce

QUESTIONS (Answer in Full Sentences)

1 Find a word which means journey.

2 Why did Tom decide not to wear his dressing gown?

3 Why did he remove a slipper?

4 What provided the light for Tom?

5 Which word tells us that the grandfather clock is old?

6 Describe three features of the garden.

7 Why did Tom feel that he had been lied to?

8 How was the door at the far end fastened?

9 How was the car garaged?

10 Why was Tom surprised when he stepped onto the doorstep?

5

The Iron Man

BY TED HUGHES

This creature had come from the depths of space, out of the heart of a star. Nobody knew what it was made of. Perhaps it could not be destroyed by any means whatsoever.

And now the space-bat-angel-dragon spoke again.

It gave the peoples of the world one week in which to prepare its first meal. They could prepare what they liked, said the dragon. But if the meal was not ready in a week, then he would start on the cities and the towns.

The peoples of the earth, the kings, the presidents and ministers, the farmers and the factory workers began to lament. Now what would happen to them? They would like to say the monster didn't exist, but how could they? There it was, covering Australia, staring out over all the countries of the world.

Now the little boy Hogarth heard all about this.

Everybody in the world was talking about it, worrying about it.

He was sure the Iron Man could do something. Compared to the space-bat-angel-dragon the Iron Man wasn't very big, of course. The Iron Man was only the size of a small tree. Nevertheless, Hogarth had faith in the Iron Man.

He visited the Iron Man in his scrap-yard, and talked to him about this great monster that was threatening the earth.

'Please,' he asked, 'please can't you think of some way of getting rid of it? If you can't, then it's the end of us all.'

The Iron Man chewed thoughtfully at his favourite titbit, a juicy, spicy old gas-stove. He shook his head slowly.

'Please think of something,' cried Hogarth. 'If this space-bat-angel-dragon licks all life off the earth, that'll be the end of your scrap iron – there'll be no people left to make it.'

The Iron Man became still. He seemed to be thinking. Suddenly his headlamps blazed red, green, blue and white all at once. And he stood up. In a great grinding voice, he gave his commands.

Hogarth danced for joy. The Iron Man had had the most stupendous idea. The Iron Man would go out, as the champion of the earth, against this monster from space.

Extract from *The Iron Man* by Ted Hughes

QUESTIONS (Answer in Full Sentences)

1 Where had the creature come from?

____

____

____

____

2 What ultimatum did the creature give the world?

____

____

____

____

3 What did he threaten to do if the meal wasn't ready?

____

____

____

____

4 Which word in the passage means to feel sad?

____

____

5 How big was the Iron Man?

6 What did the Iron Man like to chew?

7 How would you describe the Iron Man's voice? Find the word in the passage.

8 Why was Hogarth fearful?

9 Where did the Iron Man live?

10 How big was the monster?

6

The Dreamsnatcher

BY ABI ELPHINSTONE

Night deepened. Oak's camp was silent and still, as if holding its breath. Tucked up in the branches of the Sacred Oaks, they waited.

Mist slunk into the clearing below them, settling on the branches of the trees like an unwanted guest. All of the wagons had been bolted and the cobs and greyhounds tethered to trees hidden deep within the Ancientwood. Even the chickens and, on Siddy's insistence, Porridge the Second had been caged up and concealed.

The embers of a fire glowed in the middle of the clearing, turning the hanging mist to amber, and, far above this, Moll, Gryff and Alfie crouched inside the biggest of the Sacred Oaks. Siddy had been prised away into another tree to take care of his baby sister, but, on the branch below Moll, Cinderella Bull, Mooshie, Oak and their sons huddled.

Gryff leant into Moll and she ran a hand along his back. He'd keep her safe. She'd seen him leap from the tallest branches of a beech tree and land on his feet unscathed. She tucked her knees under her chin; so long as Gryff was with her, she'd be all right.

'It must be past midnight now,' Moll whispered. 'Perhaps they're not going to come after all.'

Alfie shifted beside her and the leaves on the branch trembled – as if they too knew what was coming. 'Skull will come,' he said. 'He always does.'

'And you think Cinderella Bull's plan is really going to work?'

Seconds later, it came.

At first, it was the pounding of hooves they heard; then came the feverish shrieks of the hounds. Whips cracked, shattering the stillness, and the hounds bayed louder. But there were no voices. Skull's gang were approaching the camp in a terrifying wave of silence.

Moll's palms were hot and her heart was thudding inside her. But no one moved or uttered a word within the trees, exactly as they'd planned.

The beating of hooves was louder now – and closer. Then, bursting through the mist, Moll saw the dark shapes of Skull and his gang, urging on their cobs. Six hooded shapes thundered towards them: Skull, Gobbler, Brunt, the other two boys and...

Moll's heart raced. The second Shadowmask.

The hounds rampaged through the forest and stormed into the clearing, tearing at their leashes, their teeth bleached against the night. And then suddenly they were still.

One of the riders threw back his hood; Skull's white mask hung in the mist.

'The cowards are locked inside their wagons.' His voice was brittle, like dried-out clay.

Gobbler's hunched back was a shadowy bulge in the darkness, and beside him was a man with a mask of slate, a jutting mouth and gaping eyeholes. Clumps of dead flowers for hair and poisonous berries rotting away where ears should have been...

Hemlock. And he was muttering under his breath.

Almost at once Moll felt his curse, crawling through the night to her soul, feeding on her fear. Come to us, Moll Pecksniff. You're ours now. You're not one of them. You never will be. And, so long as you stay here, you put them all in danger. Come away now; give yourself up to our curse.

Moll's mind raced. She was safe, tucked up inside the highest oak, but every fibre in her body wanted to climb down and give herself up. As if he sensed this, Gryff put two legs in front of her. His claws dug into the bark, but it would only be a matter of time before Hemlock's curse sought him out too.

Moll wanted to shake Gryff, to make him understand. What chance did any of them have against the Shadowmaster and their curses, against the Soul Splinter?

Extract from *The Dreamsnatcher* by Abi Elphinstone

QUESTIONS (Answer in Full Sentences)

1 What literary technique is used for 'trees like an unwanted guest'?

____

____

____

2 Which word in the passage means tied?

3 Which word in the passage means hidden?

4 Who would protect Moll?

5 Give the meanings of these words

unscathed

poisonous

6 What lit up the clearing?

7 Find an example of a simile in the passage.

8 Who was crouching inside the biggest Sacred Oak?

9 What 'shattered' the stillness?

10 How did Moll's body give away her fear?

7

Born to Run

BY MICHAEL MORPURGO

There was all the sudden shouting, as the ball rocketed past him into the net, and he was left diving after it despairingly, ending up flat on his face in the mud. When he looked up, there were Jimmy Rington and the others running towards him yelling and screaming: 'Loser! Loser!' Mr Butterworth said it wasn't the end of the world, but to Patrick it certainly felt like it. So Patrick had a lot of worrying to do that morning.

He was late down to breakfast as a result. He barely had time to feed Swimsy, his goldfish, and shovel down his Cocopops, before his mum was kissing him goodbye on top of his head as she passed by behind him, talking as she went, not to him at all, but to Patrick's dad, about not forgetting to get the car serviced. Then she was out of the door and gone. Minutes later Patrick was being hustled into the car, and his dad was telling him to be careful crossing the road by the school, to wait until the lollipop man said he could cross – this was what he said every morning.

Patrick was dropped off by the bridge as usual, and found himself alone at last and walking along the canal. Suddenly it didn't matter any more about Jimmy Rington or the goal he'd let in, or saying 'whatever' or Mrs Brightwell's volcanic temper tantrums. He breathed in the sweet and sour smell of the brown sauce factory. It was strange, he loved the smell, but hated the taste of the actual sauce. Shading his eyes against the sun, he looked up at the chimney to see if his kestrel was there. He wasn't, but Patrick didn't mind, because there were some ducks cruising past him, and another nearby with his bottom in the air and that always made him smile. A moorhen scurried across the towpath in front of him and disappeared into the long grass.

He hitched up his school bag and felt suddenly all bright and breezy, until he saw the swan some distance ahead of him, standing there on the towpath, looking at him, waiting for him. That worried him, because Patrick knew this swan, knew him all too well. They had met once before. It looked like the same one who had blocked his path on the way to school only a couple of weeks ago. He'd come running at Patrick wings outstretched, neck lowered to attack and hissing like a hundred snakes. Patrick had had to run into the undergrowth to escape him and had fallen into a patch of nettles. So Patrick did not like this swan, not one bit. Yet somehow he was going to have to get past him – it was the only way to get to school, and he had to get to school. The question was how to do it.

Patrick stood there eyeing the swan, just hoping that sooner rather than later the swan would decide it was time to go back into the water. But the swan stayed steadfastly where he was, glaring darkly at him, his great black feet planted firmly on the towpath. He was showing no signs of moving anywhere.

Patrick was still wondering what to do, when out of the corner of his eye he saw something floating out in the middle of the canal. It was bright green and looked plastic – a sack of some kind. He probably wouldn't have paid it any more attention – a sack's not that interesting, after all – if he hadn't heard the squeaking. It sounded as if it was coming from the sack itself, and that didn't make sense.

Patrick thought at first it might have been the piping of ducklings or moorhen chicks – he'd heard them often enough on the canal. But then he remembered that there weren't any chicks around, not any more, because it was autumn. The whole place was carpeted with yellow leaves, gold leaves, red leaves. They were all around his feet. Spring and summer were over. No, it really had to be the sack itself that was squeaking.

It was still early in the morning and Patrick's brain must have been working very slowly, because several moments passed before he realised that there was something alive inside the sack, and even then it wasn't only the squeaking that convinced him. The sack, he noticed, wasn't just drifting gently along like everything else, the leaves, the sticks, all the other flotsam in the canal. It was turning of its own accord, as if it was being propelled from inside. There was definitely something inside it, and whatever it was seemed to be struggling against the side of the plastic sack, kicking at it, trying to escape from it and squeaking in terror. He had no idea what it might be, only that it was alive and in danger of drowning. The canal wasn't that wide. It was dirty but it wasn't wide. He could do it.

Patrick didn't think about it any more. He shrugged off his school bag and leaped into the canal. He knew he was a good enough swimmer, so he wasn't worried about drowning, only about getting cold and wet. He didn't want the canal water in his mouth either, so he kept it tight shut. Just a few quick strokes out into the canal and he'd grabbed the sack, and was swimming back again. Suddenly the bank seemed a long way away, but he got there.

Climbing out was the most difficult part because his clothes were heavy and clinging, and the sack was slippery in his hands, difficult to hold on to. He felt suddenly very weak, felt the cold of the water chilling him to the bone. But with one huge effort he heaved himself up, enough to hook one leg up, on to the bank, and then he was out. Standing there, dripping from everywhere, he untied the sack and opened it. There were five puppies inside, leggy, gangly looking creatures, skeletal almost, all of them trembling with cold and crawling over one another, squirming to get out, mouths open and squeaking frantically. They were like no puppies Patrick had ever seen before.

Extract from *Born to Run* by Michael Morpurgo

QUESTIONS (Answer in Full Sentences)

1 Why did the boys call Patrick 'a loser'?

2 What was Patrick's mum reminding his dad to do?

3 What usually roosted on the chimney?

4 Find a simile about the swan.

5 Why did Patrick dislike the swan?

6 Which word describes the swan as 'unwilling to move'?

7 What attracted Patrick to the sack?

8 Why were there no chicks around?

9 What did the sack do to convince Patrick that there was something inside?

10 Why did Patrick find it difficult to climb out of the river?

11 Which word suggests that the puppies were malnourished?

12 Give an example of in the passage?

i. an adverb

ii. an adjective

iii. alliteration

8

Alone on a Wide, Wide Sea

BY MICHAEL MORPURGO

Most of the world is now too young to remember the war in Vietnam. Wars become history all too soon and are forgotten all too soon as well, before the lessons can be learned. Which is why we have more wars, and always more wars. But they are not forgotten by those who fought in them. I don't forget the anger of our guns, the shudder that went through the ship when she was hit, the silence that followed and the cries of wounded men. They called it "friendly fire" afterwards. We were bombarded by our own side, an "unfortunate" mistake they told us. It felt a little more than unfortunate at the time. Good men died for nothing that day, and I was lucky not to be one of them.

These were times I do remember, only too well, but don't want to have to think about. I don't want to write about them either, but I can't pass by Vietnam as if it never happened, as if I'd never been there, been part of it. Not because I'm proud of it. On the contrary.

There were long months of boredom at sea, long nights sweating below deck. I can still remember how excitement turned to fear in my stomach when the guns first fired. I can still see Dickie Donnelly from Adelaide – we only just celebrated his eighteenth birthday – lying there on the deck, his eyes looking up at the sky above him and not seeing. There wasn't a mark on him. It must have been the blast that killed him. I was holding his hand when I felt the last breath of life go out of him.

But, apart from Dickie Donnelly, most of the dying in the war was done far away, on the shore. I discovered it's a whole lot easier to do your killing when you're miles away from your target. You're in your ship, way out at sea, and you just fire the guns. You don't see where the shells land. So you don't think about it, because you don't have to, at least not to start with, not until you come face to face with it. After Dickie Donnelly, I couldn't put it out of my mind. This was what our shells were doing to the enemy, to the Vietcong, to the North Vietnamese. They'd be young lads, just like Dickie, with mothers and fathers, sisters and brothers, an enemy I'd never even seen. And I was firing the guns that did it. All I'd ever done while I'd been at sea, it seemed to me, was killing.

I couldn't wait for the war to end, to get out of the navy. Sickened and sad I turned my back on the sea, forever I hoped. I had come to hate the sea, the place I'd always loved, where I'd always longed to be. For me the sea had become a place of blood.

I went inland after the navy, bummed my way around, picking up any work I could find. I went gold mining in Western Australia, worked on a cattle station in the Northern Territories, spent most of my time branding cattle. I did seasonal work picking grapes in vineyards outside Adelaide, in the Clare Valley it was. And after that, I was a jackaroo for a while on a sheep station near Armidale in New South Wales. After that I never wanted to look at another sheep in my life. Back-breaking work, smelly work. At times I felt like I was back on Cooper's Station.

I couldn't settle anywhere, not for long. I kept moving on, moving on. I wasn't leaving anywhere. I wasn't going anywhere. I was just drifting. I still wore Kitty's key around my neck, never took it off, not once. But I'd long since stopped believing it was lucky. I wore it, mostly out of habit, and maybe because I still thought that I might one day be able to go back to England and find Kitty, find out if she'd ever existed even, find out what the key was for.

But I never did it, and I know why. I was frightened, frightened of discovering the worst – that she never had existed, that I'd made her up so as not to feel entirely alone in this world. I still thought about the key though, when I caught sight of it in the mirror as I was shaving. I thought about it every time I touched it. But any real hope I had harboured of actually ever doing anything about it was fast fading, along with my sanity. My centre would not hold.

I don't know why it happened when it did. None of it really makes much sense to me even now. If there was a physical cause that triggered my troubles – and when it comes to health, I don't think body and mind can be separated – then it might well have been lack of sleep. No matter how exhausted I was after a day's work, I couldn't get to sleep. I'd lie there, not tossing and turning, just thinking. And no matter how hard I tried, my mind kept coming back to it. It was always the killing. It was the shining tuna lying on the deck bleeding, fighting for life, Dickie Donnelly's last breath warm on my hand.

But there was another picture there that haunted me, that would not go away every time I closed my eyes. I'd seen it first as a black and white photo in a magazine, I think, then in a film on television. It was an image of a young girl in Vietnam, running down the road away from her village. She had been burned by napalm bombing, dreadfully burned. She needed help. She was coming towards me. She was naked and she was crying. And she kept coming towards me, holding out her arms to me, and suddenly her face would be Kitty's face. I knew I'd been part of the war that had done that to her, to a girl just like Kitty and to thousands and thousands of others too. Every night she was there, and every night I couldn't sleep.

I'd be late for work in the morning, or I'd fall asleep on the job. I'd get the sack. Time and again I got the sack. Any money I did earn I'd gamble away the same day I got it. I'd hitch a ride anywhere and had no idea where I was when I arrived nor why I'd gone there. I felt myself slipping into a deep dark hole of despair. I couldn't find any way of stopping myself, and in the end I didn't even want to stop myself. It seemed a lot easier just to give up and let go. So I did.

Extract from Alone on a Wide, Wide Sea by Michael Morpurgo

QUESTIONS (Answer in Full Sentences)

1 How does the author remember the war? Give two examples.

i. ______________________________

ii. ______________________________

2 Why did the author's excitement turn to fear?

____

____

____

3 What was the author doing when Dickie Donnelly died?

____

____

____

____

4 Which country was Dickie from?

5 Why did the author hate the sea?

6 Name three types of jobs the author did after the war?

i.

ii.

iii.

7 What did the author wear around his neck?

8 Where was Kitty from?

9 What image haunted the author?

10 Why did the author get the sack?

11 Which word at the end of the passage tells you the author was distressed?

Answers

1 The Iron Man

1. He uses short sentences and repetition
2. A house
3. His great iron head, shaped like a dustbin, like a crab on its back
4. Vulnerable, wary, frightened, apprehensive
5. The sound of the sea
6. Like a crab on its back
7. The wind sang through his iron finger
8. Just before dawn
9. They had to feed their chicks
10. A clam

2 Once

1. Paper
2. To reassure him
3. It was rotten
4. They pushed the wood through
5. The train tracks and countryside
6. So that they can escape
7. He tells them a story
8. Should portray anxiety, sadness, fear
9. A carrot
10. Soldiers

3 The Firework-Maker's Daughter

1. He sent his courtiers a White Elephant to punish them
2. He had expensive taste
3. Silk sheets, mango flavoured Turkish Delight, tusks gold leafed
4. Chulak
5. Bangkok Wanderers for the Cup, Chang loves Lotus Blossom, Eat at the Golden Lantern, Star of India Tandoori House
6. Because no one else knew he could talk
7. Quivering
8. With charcoal and paint
9. Chulake wanted to make money
10. Like a ton of strawberry ice cream

4 Tom's Midnight Garden

1. Expedition
2. It was too hot
3. To wedge the door open
4. The moon
5. Ancient
6. Lawn, flower beds, fir tree, greenhouse, path
7. Because they told him the outside space is poky
8. With a bolt
9. With tarpaulin
10. He was surprised at the sight of the garden

5 The Iron Man

1. The heart of a star
2. One week to prepare its first meal
3. He would destroy the cities and towns
4. Lament
5. The size of a small tree
6. Metal
7. Grinding
8. That the creature would destroy the earth
9. In a scrap yard
10. As big as Australia

6 The Dreamsnatcher

1. Simile
2. Tethered
3. Concealed
4. Gryff
5. Unharmed, causing illness
6. The embers of a fire
7. Trees like an unwanted guest, his voice was brittle like dried out clay
8. Moll, Gryff and Alfie
9. Whips cracked
10. Her heart raced and her palms were hot

7 Born to Run

1. Because he let a ball in the goal
2. To get the car serviced
3. A kestrel
4. Hissing like a hundred snakes
5. Because he fell into a patch of nettles when he escaped
6. Steadfastly
7. He heard squeaking
8. It was autumn
9. The sack was turning
10. His clothes were heavy
11. Skeletal
12. **(i) Adverbs:** ¬ly¬ words. **(ii) Adjective:** bright, yellow, gold, heavy, weak, sweet, sour.
    (iii) Alliteration: sudden shouting

8 Alone on the Wide, Wide Sea

1. **(i)** The cries of the wounded men
   (ii) The shudder of the guns
2. When the guns were first fired
3. Holding his hand
4. Australia
5. It had become a place of blood
6. **(i)** worked on a cattle station **(ii)** goldmining
   (iii) picking grapes / jackaroo on a sheep farm
7. Kitty's key
8. England
9. The image of the Vietnamese girl badly burned
10. He would be late for work or fall asleep on the job
11. Despair

Recommended book list for 10-12 year olds

These books have all been personally read by the author and shared with her many pupils over the years. All the titles will appeal to both boys and girls.

Once
by Morris Gleitzman

Goodnight Mister Tom
by Michelle Magorian

Carrie's War
by Nina Bawden

Flour Babies
by Anne Fine

War Horse
by Michael Morpurgo

Private Peaceful
by Michael Morpurgo

Flamingo Boy
by Michael Morpurgo

Shadow
by Michael Morpurgo

Born to Run
by Michael Morpurgo

Kensuke's Kingdom
by Michael Morpurgo

Kaspar
by Michael Morpurgo

Varjak Paw
by SF Said

The Outlaw Varjak Paw
by SF Said

Holes
by Louis Sachar

Northern Lights
by Philip Pullman

The Subtle Knife
by Philip Pullman

Continued...

Recommended book list for 9 -12 year olds

The Amber Spyglass
by Philip Pullman

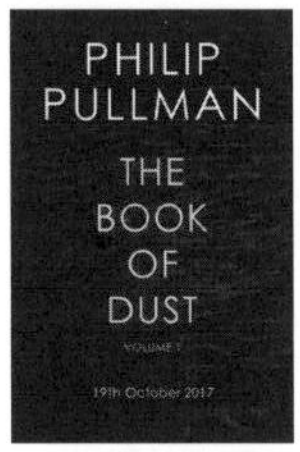

The Book of Dust
by Philip Pullman

Clockwork
by Philip Pullman

Tom's Midnight Garden
by Philippa Pearce

The Hobbit
by JRR Tolkien

I am David
by Anne Holm

Dreamsnatcher
by Abi Elphinstone

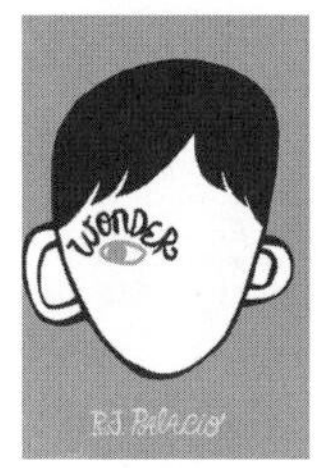

Wonder
by RJ Palacio

Street Child
by Berlie Doherty

Chinese Cinderella
by Adeline Yen Mah

Journey to the River Sea
by Eva Ibbotson

Skellig
by David Almond

The Lion, the Witch and the Wardrobe
by CS Lewis

Harry Potter and the Philosopher's Stone
by JK Rowling